CHARLES
DREW

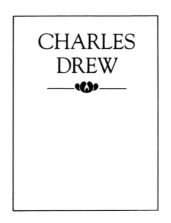

CHARLES DREW

❧

Robyn Mahone-Lonesome

Senior Consulting Editor
Nathan Irvin Huggins
Director
W.E.B. Du Bois Institute for Afro-American Research
Harvard University

CHELSEA HOUSE PUBLISHERS
Philadelphia

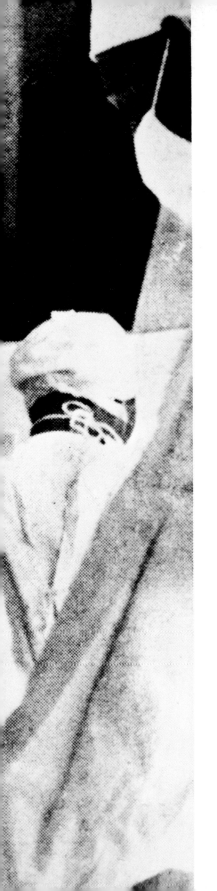

CHELSEA HOUSE PUBLISHERS
Editor-in-Chief Nancy Toff
Executive Editor Remmel T. Nunn
Managing Editor Karyn Gullen Browne
Copy Chief Juliann Barbato
Picture Editor Adrian G. Allen
Art Director Maria Epes
Manufacturing Manager Gerald Levine

Black Americans of Achievement
Senior Editor Richard Rennert

Staff for CHARLES DREW
Copy Editor Brian Sookram
Deputy Copy Chief Nicole Bowen
Editorial Assistant Navorn Johnson
Picture Researcher Lisa Kirchner
Assistant Art Director Loraine Machlin
Designer Ghila Krajzman
Production Manager Joseph Romano
Production Coordinator Marie Claire Cebrián
Cover Illustration Robert Caputo

9 8

Library of Congress Cataloging-in-Publication Data
Mahone-Lonesome, Robyn.
Charles R. Drew / Robyn Mahone-Lonesome.
p. cm.—(Black Americans of achievement)
Bibliography: p.
Includes index.
Summary: A biography of the surgeon who conducted research on the
properties and preservation of blood plasma and was a leader in estab-
lishing blood banks.
ISBN 1-55546-581-1
      0-7910-0237-2 (pbk.)
1. Drew, Charles Richard, 1904–1950. 2. Surgeons—United
States—Biography. 3. Afro-American surgeons—United States—
Biography. [1. Drew, Charles Richard, 1904–1950. 2. Physi-
cians. 3. Afro-Americans—Biography.] I. Title. II. Series.
RD27.35.D74M34 1990   89-9862
617'.092—dc20   CIP
[B]   AC

CONTENTS

BLACK AMERICANS OF ACHIEVEMENT

HENRY AARON
baseball great

KAREEM ABDUL-JABBAR
basketball great

MUHAMMAD ALI
heavyweight champion

RICHARD ALLEN
*religious leader and
social activist*

MAYA ANGELOU
author

LOUIS ARMSTRONG
musician

ARTHUR ASHE
tennis great

JOSEPHINE BAKER
entertainer

JAMES BALDWIN
author

BENJAMIN BANNEKER
scientist and mathematician

AMIRI BARAKA
poet and playwright

COUNT BASIE
bandleader and composer

ROMARE BEARDEN
artist

JAMES BECKWOURTH
frontiersman

MARY McLEOD BETHUNE
educator

GEORGE WASHINGTON
CARVER
botanist

CHARLES CHESNUTT
author

BILL COSBY
entertainer

PAUL CUFFE
merchant and abolitionist

MILES DAVIS
musician

FATHER DIVINE
religious leader

FREDERICK DOUGLASS
abolitionist editor

CHARLES DREW
physician

W. E. B. DU BOIS
scholar and activist

PAUL LAURENCE DUNBAR
poet

DUKE ELLINGTON
bandleader and composer

RALPH ELLISON
author

JULIUS ERVING
basketball great

LOUIS FARRAKHAN
political activist

ELLA FITZGERALD
singer

MARCUS GARVEY
black nationalist leader

JOSH GIBSON
baseball great

WHOOPI GOLDBERG
entertainer

ALEX HALEY
author

PRINCE HALL
social reformer

JIMI HENDRIX
musician

MATTHEW HENSON
explorer

BILLIE HOLIDAY
singer

LENA HORNE
entertainer

WHITNEY HOUSTON
singer and actress

LANGSTON HUGHES
poet

ZORA NEALE HURSTON
author

JESSE JACKSON
civil-rights leader and politician

MICHAEL JACKSON
entertainer

JACK JOHNSON
heavyweight champion

MAGIC JOHNSON
basketball great

SCOTT JOPLIN
composer

BARBARA JORDAN
politician

MICHAEL JORDAN
basketball great

CORETTA SCOTT KING
civil-rights leader

MARTIN LUTHER KING, JR.
civil-rights leader

LEWIS LATIMER
scientist

SPIKE LEE
filmmaker

CARL LEWIS
champion athlete

JOE LOUIS
heavyweight champion

RONALD McNAIR
astronaut

MALCOLM X
militant black leader

BOB MARLEY
musician

THURGOOD MARSHALL
Supreme Court justice

TONI MORRISON
author

ELIJAH MUHAMMAD
religious leader

EDDIE MURPHY
entertainer

JESSE OWENS
champion athlete

SATCHEL PAIGE
baseball great

CHARLIE PARKER
musician

ROSA PARKS
civil-rights leader

COLIN POWELL
military leader

PAUL ROBESON
singer and actor

JACKIE ROBINSON
baseball great

DIANA ROSS
entertainer

WILL SMITH
actor

CLARENCE THOMAS
Supreme Court Justice

SOJOURNER TRUTH
antislavery activist

HARRIET TUBMAN
antislavery activist

NAT TURNER
slave revolt leader

DENMARK VESEY
slave revolt leader

ALICE WALKER
author

MADAM C. J. WALKER
entrepreneur

BOOKER T. WASHINGTON
educator

DENZEL WASHINGTON
actor

OPRAH WINFREY
entertainer

TIGER WOODS
golf star

RICHARD WRIGHT
author

ON ACHIEVEMENT

Coretta Scott King

BEFORE YOU BEGIN this book, I hope you will ask yourself what the word *excellence* means to you. I think that it's a question we should all ask and keep asking as we grow older and change. Because the truest answer to it should never change. When you think of excellence, perhaps you think of success at work; or of becoming wealthy; or meeting the right person, getting married, and having a good family life.

Those important goals are worth striving for, but there is a better way to look at excellence. As Martin Luther King, Jr., said in one of his last sermons, "I want you to be first in love. I want you to be first in moral excellence. I want you to be first in generosity. If you want to be important, wonderful. If you want to be great, wonderful. But recognize that he who is greatest among you shall be your servant."

My husband, Martin Luther King, Jr., knew that the true meaning of achievement is service. When I met him, in 1952, he was already ordained as a Baptist preacher and was working toward a doctoral degree at Boston University. I was studying at the New England Conservatory and dreamed of accomplishments in music. We married a year later, and after I graduated the following year we moved to Montgomery, Alabama. We didn't know it then, but our notions of achievement were about to undergo a dramatic change.

You may have read or heard about what happened next. What began with the boycott of a local bus line grew into a national movement, and by the time he was assassinated in 1968 my husband had fashioned a black movement powerful enough to shatter forever the practice of racial seg- regation. What you may not have read about is where he got his method for resisting injustice without compromising his religious beliefs.

7

He adopted the strategy of nonviolence from a man of a different race, who lived in a distant country, and even practiced a different religion. The man was Mahatma Gandhi, the great leader of India, who devoted his life to serving humanity in the spirit of love and nonviolence. It was in these principles that Martin discovered his method for social reform. More than anything else, those two principles were the key to his achievements.

This book is about black Americans who served society through the excellence of their achievements. It forms a part of the rich history of black men and women in America—a history of stunning accomplishments in every field of human endeavor, from literature and art to science, industry, education, diplomacy, athletics, jurisprudence, even polar exploration.

Not all of the people in this history had the same ideals, but I think you will find something that all of them have in common. Like Martin Luther King, Jr., they all decided to become "drum majors" and serve humanity. In that principle—whether it was expressed in books, inventions, or song—they found something outside themselves to use as a goal and a guide. Something that showed them a way to serve others, instead of living only for themselves.

Reading the stories of these courageous men and women not only helps us discover the principles that we will use to guide our own lives but also teaches us about our black heritage and about America itself. It is crucial for us to know the heroes and heroines of our history and to realize that the price we paid in our struggle for equality in America was dear. But we must also understand that we have gotten as far as we have partly because America's democratic system and ideals made it possible.

We are still struggling with racism and prejudice. But the great men and women in this series are a tribute to the spirit of our democratic ideals and the system in which they have flourished. And that makes their stories special and worth knowing. ❧

CHARLES
DREW

1

BLOOD
FOR
BRITAIN

◆◆◆

ON JULY 16, 1940, during the early stages of World War II, the German chancellor Adolf Hitler told his military advisers, "I have decided to begin to prepare for, and if necessary to carry out, an invasion of England." One month later, Nazi Germany, in its attempt to gain global supremacy, took the first steps in launching an all-out offensive against its chief rival, Great Britain. German planes crossed the English Channel to raid British airfields and form an air blockade. Boasting more than 2,000 aircraft, the German Luftwaffe outnumbered Britain's Royal Air Force (RAF) by about 1,400 planes, and Nazi Stukas and Messerschmitt 109s and 110s soon drove the RAF out of the sky over southern England.

Then the attacks grew worse. On the afternoon of September 7, the Germans carried out a massive strike on London. An initial group of 320 Nazi bombers flew over the channel and up the Thames River, blasting a British arsenal, power stations, and docks. The assault continued deep into the night, with 250

German bombers began assaulting London, England, in the summer of 1940 with a series of quick yet devastating air strikes that the British termed "the Blitz." These sudden attacks, which left England in desperate need of large supplies of blood to administer to its wounded, were instrumental in prompting Drew to organize the world's first comprehensive blood-banking program.

twin-engine bombers guided to their targets by fires that were still blazing from the previous bombings. The Luftwaffe pressed the attack until dawn, then resumed the onslaught at twilight. By the end of September 8, the strikes had killed 842 Londoners. Moreover, the besieged city, the German high command announced, was "a sea of flames."

The devastating attacks on London continued every night for the next four weeks. During each of the Luftwaffe assaults, an average of 165 planes dropped 13,600 tons of explosives and left much of

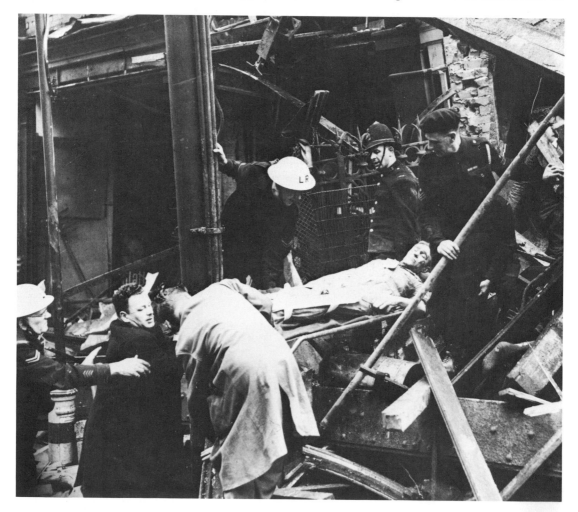

London a smoldering heap of death and destruction. These lightning attacks, termed "the Blitz" by the British people, also resulted in a large number of wounded civilians, many of them in desperate need of blood transfusions.

Unfortunately, England's medical community did not have enough blood to go around, for blood banking was still in its early stages. In 1940, most physicians were aware that the whole blood used in transfusions could be stored for only a few days. After

British civilians wounded during the Blitz (above and opposite) receive treatment amid the rubble created by Nazi Germany's air attacks. Scenes like these spurred the medical community to investigate the use of blood substitutes in transfusions because whole blood, normally employed in such procedures, can be safely stored for only a brief period.

John Beattie, a former teacher of Drew's, was placed in charge of England's blood collection program during World War II. When America's Blood Transfusion Betterment Association set up its own Blood for Britain program in 1940, Beattie cabled the following recommendation to the organization: UNIFORM STANDARDS FOR ALL BLOOD BANKS OF UTMOST IMPORTANCE. SUGGEST YOU APPOINT OVERALL DIRECTOR IF PROGRAM IS TO CONTINUE. SUGGEST CHARLES R. DREW IF AVAILABLE.

that, the red corpuscles, which carry oxygen to the body's tissues, would begin to break down. Accordingly, the medical community was exploring the use of blood plasma (the fluid part of blood, which contains nutrients, proteins, antibodies, and hormones) as a substitute for whole blood during transfusions.

Blood plasma, which can be stored for longer periods than whole blood, does not contain any red corpuscles. Thus, it is not a long-term substitute for whole blood. But it is usually transfused with few complications and can sustain the recipient until whole blood is available.

John Beattie, director of England's Army Blood Transfusion Service, was charged with initiating a major blood collection program for his country's wounded. Britain, however, was under siege and needed assistance in setting up such a program. Wasting little time, Beattie turned to the United States for help.

At his behest, members of America's Blood Transfusion Betterment Association quickly summoned the nation's leading experts on blood preservation to a meeting that summer in New York City. Beattie oversaw the conference, which was also attended by representatives of the American Red Cross, the National Research Council, the army surgeon general's office, and commercial laboratories. The meeting covered all facets of the proposal to supply blood to Britain. Blood collection centers had to be established, the collected blood had to be processed, and then it had to be shipped overseas. Much organizational work was required for the first great experiment in mass production of human plasma.

A Blood for Britain program was finally established in early August 1940, after 11 such meetings. But the first shipment of blood plasma sent overseas never reached its destination. A German torpedo sank the vessel carrying the medical supplies.

More problems followed. Few donors turned out for the Blood for Britain program, and much of the plasma that did reach England was contaminated and therefore unusable. It became increasingly obvious to Beattie that someone was needed immediately to take charge of the program. John Scudder, an assistant professor of clinical surgery at Columbia University in New York City and a physician at the nearby

Columbia Presbyterian Hospital, was asked to fill the position of supervisor. When he declined the post, it was offered to one of his former students, Charles Drew, who had also been one of Beattie's pupils.

Drew, a 36-year-old black physician, was not a unanimous choice for program director. Even the Blood Transfusion Betterment Association, which felt he was "the best qualified of anyone we know to act in this important development," noted that naming him to the supervisory post might cause additional problems for the blood-banking program because he was black. There seemed to be too much racial prejudice and legalized discrimination in the United States for him to have any real power.

But Beattie and others maintained that Drew was indeed the best person for the job. A teacher at the medical college of Howard University in Washington, D.C., Drew was the first black in America to receive the degree of Doctor of Science in Medicine. He was widely recognized as an expert surgeon and an adept organizer. Moreover, he had extensively researched blood banking and was one of the nation's leading authorities on the subject. Few people were as qualified for the position.

In late September, Drew received permission from Howard University to take a leave of absence and become the medical supervisor of the Blood for Britain program. By that time, he had already been in touch with Beattie. The first shipment of plasma had been sent to England in mid-August, and Beattie had contacted Drew a few weeks later, asking his former student, "Could you secure five thousand ampoules dried plasma for transfusion work immediately and follow this by equal quantity in three to four weeks? Contents each ampoule should represent about one pint whole plasma." Although Drew was not yet in a position to act on Beattie's request, he said later,

"It was that cablegram which really mobilized American aid."

Drew's chief responsibilities as head of the Blood for Britain program were to devise a standard procedure for collecting blood from the donors and processing the blood plasma to ensure the safety of the recipients. He came up with the idea of using mobile units with refrigeration facilities to collect blood. He also made sure that all the blood was sent to a central

Taking over the reins of America's Blood for Britain program in September 1940, Drew researched the results of laboratory experiments carried out by other blood specialists and turned his findings into a method for mass-producing human plasma, the fluid part of blood. Making use of modified cream separators was one of the ways he speeded up the process of obtaining plasma from whole blood.

Blood plasma is administered to a wounded American soldier during World War II. "When your blood flows into the veins of a wounded soldier that soldier knows it is more than medicine for his body," said one U.S. Army general. "It is a part of you that you are giving to help keep him alive."

laboratory, where the processing and sterilization of the blood plasma could be carefully monitored. As soon as the plasma was separated from the blood cells, the water in the plasma evaporated but the proteins remained. The resulting product, dried plasma, was then frozen in sealed packets for easy storage and delivery.

Drew's efforts, according to the American Red Cross, were astounding. In reporting on his work, the association said that Drew "brought together, for the benefit of hematologists everywhere, the latest knowledge acquired by scientists working in several fields." He showed "exceptional ability in synthesizing the work of others—in selecting from a multiplicity of diverse and often contradictory findings those which had practical application to the problems at hand."

The Blood for Britain program, operating solely in New York, managed to collect 14,500 pints of blood plasma. The program remained intact through January 1941. By then, the British had established their own plasma collection program based on Drew's methods, and the Blood Transfusion Betterment Association was told that its plasma was no longer needed.

But Drew's work with plasma collection was not yet over. At the request of the American armed forces, the Blood Transfusion Betterment Association, in conjunction with the National Research Council and the American Red Cross, immediately continued the collection program to supply the country's needs. Drew was named assistant director of blood procurement for the national program and was appointed head of New York City's Red Cross blood bank. By the time the United States formally entered World War II in late 1941, blood donor stations were already in place around the nation and at strategic points overseas.

The Allies' campaign against Nazi Germany and its Axis partners ultimately turned out to be the bloodiest conflict in world history. Nearly 50 million people died in the war. But countless more would have perished had it not been for the extraordinary contributions of Charles Drew, a tireless pioneer in trying times. ✺

2

"A DIME A DOZEN"

───── ✦ ─────

CHARLES RICHARD DREW was born into a middle-class household in Washington, D.C., on June 3, 1904. His father, Richard, was a carpet layer who worked for the Moses Furniture Company and served as financial secretary for the local branch of the Carpet, Linoleum, and Soft Tile-Layers Union. An outspoken man who was clearly the head of the house, he refused to let his wife, Nora, a graduate of nearby Howard University and a former schoolteacher, accept another job. Her role was to take care of the five Drew children, of whom the eldest was Charlie, followed by Elsie, Joseph, Nora, and Eva.

The Drews were a closely knit family. They had lived with Richard's parents until 1908, when they moved to the house where Charlie had been born: a three-story residence owned by his maternal grandparents and located in a racially mixed community called Foggy Bottom because it was often enveloped by mist from the Potomac River. The Drews resided in this 16-room house at 1806 E Street for 6 years, then moved to another building down the block.

For a young black such as Charlie, Foggy Bottom was an especially good neighborhood in which to grow up. During the days of slavery a half century earlier, a large number of free blacks had settled in the nation's capital because it was the only southern city in which they were allowed to establish a separate middle-class society complete with its own schools,

Drew at the age of about six months. He spent most of his youth in a racially mixed neighborhood in Washington, D.C.

Drew's father, Richard (left), and mother, Nora (right), had a mixed racial heritage. Their ancestry was partly Native American, Scottish, and English, as well as African.

clubs, businesses, and churches. In effect, the black bourgeoisie of Washington, D.C., created a self-contained world. Whereas most southern blacks suffered from the effects of the federally sanctioned segregation laws known as Jim Crow laws, the black residents of Foggy Bottom lived as comfortably as most middle-class whites.

The Drews' ties to the local black community were strengthened at the Nineteenth Street Baptist Church, which they attended regularly. There they listened to the Reverend Walter Brooks tell his parishioners that they should serve the community. "All of the family was influenced by this minister," Charlie's sister Nora recalled. Their mother was a deaconess at the church, and their father, who played the piano and the guitar at home, sang in its choir.

Like Richard Drew, Charlie was extremely resolute. A freckle-faced, curly-haired youth with an easy smile, he began hawking newspapers on a street corner a few years after he entered Stevens Elementary

Drew (second from right) with his sisters Elsie (right) and Nora and brother, Joseph. A fifth child, Eva, was born when Charlie was 17 years old.

School. Shortly after his brother, Joe, joined him in selling copies of the *Washington Times and Herald*, Charlie decided to expand their operation. He arranged for six other youths to work for them as newsboys, posting themselves directly outside office buildings at the end of each workday so that they could come into contact with a large number of customers.

When Charlie got a little older and stopped selling newspapers, he found work at construction sites. Even though his family was fairly well off, his parents always expected their children to hold a job. "Don't you ever forget," the Drew youngsters were lectured by their mother, "that you were cared for and educated by your father [who worked] on his knees."

In 1918, Charlie graduated from elementary school and enrolled in Dunbar High School, which was named after Paul Laurence Dunbar, the first black American poet to gain international recognition. A segregated school, Dunbar High had the reputation of being one of the best public schools for blacks in the entire nation. Indeed, Dunbar saw more of its graduates go to college than any other high school in Washington, D.C.

Encouraged by his parents to excel scholastically, Charlie flourished at Dunbar. He was an excellent student, but he proved to be even better at sports than he was in the classroom. He had shown outstanding athletic prowess as early as age five, when he won an annual swimming competition in his neighborhood—an event that he went on to win for five consecutive years.

Charlie proved to be an extraordinary athlete for all seasons at Dunbar. He starred on the football team in the fall, played basketball in the winter, and ran track and was also on the baseball team in the spring. For two successive years, he was awarded the James E. Walker Memorial Medal for being the school's top

Like most blacks in Washington, D.C., Drew grew up in relative comfort and safety, especially when compared with the experiences of blacks in other American cities. Because blacks in the nation's capital had formed their own middle class, he rarely suffered from the effects of segregation laws.

all-around athlete. His classmates not only cited him as Best Athlete when he was a senior but also voted him Most Popular and the Student Who Has Done Most for the School. In his final year of high school, he was also named captain of Company B in the Third Regiment of the High School Cadet Corps, a military training establishment.

Charlie encountered his share of sorrows in high school. His sister Elsie died from tuberculosis in the spring of 1920—a tragic loss that influenced his de-

cision to study medicine. His family pulled up its roots
in Foggy Bottom later in the year and moved away
from the neighborhood, crossing the Potomac and
settling in a two-story house in Arlington, Virginia.
But instead of transferring to a school that was nearby,
he remained at Dunbar and graduated from there in
1922.

Drew at the age of 16, with the Dunbar High School football team (back row, third from right). His athletic prowess helped him win a partial scholarship to Amherst College in Massachusetts.

Drew's outstanding athletic record in high school helped him win a partial scholarship to one of the nation's leading liberal arts institutions: Amherst College in Massachusetts. He quickly learned, however, that he had not been awarded the scholarship just because he was good at sports. Within the first few months of his freshman year, he was summoned

Drew (back row, far left) with the Dunbar High School basketball team.

to the dean's office and told that his grades were disappointing. Perhaps, the dean suggested, Drew's involvement in a variety of athletic activities was keeping him from studying as hard as he should.

Drew replied that his interest in sports was not the cause of his difficulties. Rather, his poor showing probably had something to do with his coming from a segregated high school, where he may not have received a first-rate education.

Dunbar was a fine school, the dean countered. In fact, Amherst accepted students from Dunbar without asking them to take an entrance exam to indicate their level of learning.

The dean then urged Drew to think about his career goals. If he wanted to pursue athletics as a career, he should work toward that end. But if he wanted to realize his full potential and use his brain as well as his brawn, he might find it more rewarding. "Mr. Drew," the dean said in concluding their interview, "Negro athletes are a dime a dozen."

3

HIGH
HURDLES

I NTENT ON BECOMING a doctor, Drew quickly improved his study habits. But the 6-foot-1, 195-pounder refused to give up athletics at Amherst, where football and track were his best sports. "He could have played regular on any team in the country," the school's football coach D. O. ("Tuss") McLaughry said. "He was lightning on the getaway and dynamite on inside plays, plowing on with a 'second effort' that brought him yardage long after he should have been stopped. He threw the old pumpkin-shaped ball farther and with more accuracy than anyone else I ever saw, and was also an excellent receiver. He was equally effective on defense, a true tackler and pass stopper."

Both as a junior (when he won the Thomas W. Ashley Memorial Trophy for being the football team's most valuable player) and as a senior, Drew received an honorable mention as an all-American for his play at halfback. Making the big play seemed to come naturally to him. During the championship game against Wesleyan in 1925, he ran a kickoff for a touchdown, then threw a 35-yard pass in the closing seconds of the final quarter for the winning score. "A storybook game if ever I saw one," recalled W. Montague Cobb, a classmate who later became professor of anatomy at the predominantly black Howard University.

Drew at Amherst College during his sophomore year, when he became the star running back on the school's football team. Two years later, his outstanding play made him a candidate for all-American honors.

31

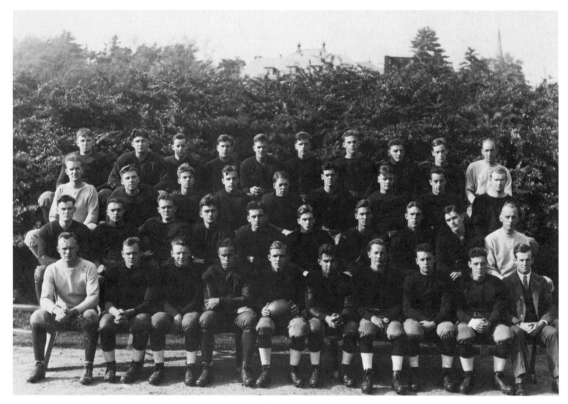

Drew with the Amherst College football team (above; front row, fourth from left) and track team (opposite; front row, center). The hard work, discipline, and sense of teamwork that he displayed as an athlete were also traits he exhibited as a physician.

Drew's football heroics were matched by his outstanding performances in track. His premier events were the high jump and the 120-yard high hurdles, in which he set a school record of 15.2 seconds and won a national championship. Consequently, there was little surprise when he was elected captain of the team during his senior year, or when he was presented with the Howard Hill Mossman Cup, an award for "bringing the greatest honor in athletics" to Amherst, in 1926.

But not everything went smoothly with Drew. Years later, his wife, Lenore, noted that even though he was an outstanding athlete "a great many people weren't ready for black stars in a white world, and he met with racial slurs both on and off the field. The insults made him flush the dangerous, dark-red color that earned him the nickname 'Big Red.' "

Drew, however, always maintained his composure, she said. "He had already decided that our people— any people—could make more progress by 'doing and showing' than by any amount of violent demonstration."

Perhaps the biggest hurdle Drew faced at Amherst occurred far away from the roar of the crowd. The trying situation arose one Saturday during the football season in his junior year, when he was being hit especially hard by the opposing team every time he carried the ball. Finally, on yet another running play, he broke free from the defense, dodging several tacklers on his way to the goal line. He was almost there when two defenders knocked him down.

While he was being tackled, Drew managed to fall forward into the end zone for a touchdown. But he felt a sharp pain when he hit the turf. Several

D. O. ("Tuss") McLaughry, the football coach at Amherst College, said that "as a football player, Drew was great. He could have played regular on any team in the country, both in his era, and anytime since."

cleats from the football shoe of one of his tacklers had sunk into Drew's thigh. The players untangled quickly and pulled the cleats out. The part of Drew's uniform that surrounded the gaping wound immediately turned deep red.

Drew's thigh injury became quite serious when the wound showed signs of infection, and he had to be hospitalized. There was even a possibility that he would lose the leg if the infection could not be contained. But his doctor assured him that he had nothing to worry about. Modern medicine worked wonders. Although there would be a walnut-sized indentation in his thigh for the rest of his life, his leg would completely recover from the injury.

To help cheer up the premedical student while he was convalescing, the physician invited Drew to look in on another patient, a 16 year old who immediately recognized the star athlete from his photographs in the sports pages. The teenager had read the newspaper accounts of Drew's injury and wanted to know if he would be able to play football next season. Drew assured the worried fan that he would be ready.

Then the doctor pulled back the covers on the young man's bed. Drew watched as the physician removed a bandage that was taped to the teenager's abdomen. Two incisions had been made in his body. A plastic tube, with a big safety pin at the end, stuck out from the left incision. It was a drainage tube, the doctor said, and the pin prevented the tube from slipping into the abdomen.

The physician unfastened the pin, and the unpleasant odor of bodily fluids immediately filled the room. He drained the abdomen before cleaning the incision with a medicated salve. Then he pointed to the right incision. That was where an appendectomy had been performed, the doctor told Drew. The young man's appendix had ruptured—a malady that had nearly proved fatal. The unhealthy organ had been removed, but the operation had not gone as easily as the doctor desired, and it had been necessary to transfuse blood during the surgery. The hospital's supply of blood was low, however, and there had barely been enough.

As he followed the physician on his rounds, Drew became convinced that he should make medicine his

career. Years later, he acknowledged as much when he said, "I got banged up in football and wanted to know how the body works." Yet he was well aware of how difficult it was to become a doctor, especially for a black American.

Lucas Santomée, who lived in the colony of New Amsterdam in the 1660s, is generally regarded as the New World's first black physician. More than a century later, James Derham of New Orleans, Louisiana, gained renown as the first black doctor to be trained in America. In the 1830s, the American Colonization Society, a group founded on the belief that the

The commencement ceremonies at Amherst in 1926. After graduating from college that year, Drew set his sights on attending Howard Medical College in Washington, D.C. His application to Howard was rejected on a technicality, however, prompting him to vow, "Someday I'll come back here and run this damned place."

best way to achieve black freedom was to resettle former slaves in Africa, helped a few blacks train as physicians so they could be of service in the West African colony of Liberia. David Peck became the first black in America to receive a medical degree, graduating from Rush Medical College in 1847.

The first black medical schools to be established in the United States were Howard Medical College in Washington, D.C., which opened in 1868, and Meharry Medical College in Nashville, Tennessee, which began accepting students eight years later. By the 1920s, there were roughly 30 other black medical

Drew spent the two years following his graduation from Amherst by working as the coach of the Morgan College basketball team (below; back row, far right) and manager of a local swimming pool (opposite). By 1928, he had saved enough money to enroll in medical school. .

schools in the country. Most of them, however, were very small. Eighty percent of the approximately 2,500 students who were enrolled in black medical schools attended either Howard Medical College or Meharry Medical College. Only 600 black medical students were enrolled in predominantly white institutions. For the most part, desegregated schools did not actively seek blacks for their programs.

When Drew graduated from Amherst in 1926 with the idea of applying to medical school, he

planned on attending Howard Medical College, which was located in his old hometown. He knew that living at home while he attended the school would help him save money. Indeed, scraping together enough money to pay his tuition was a problem. His father offered to help out somewhat, but he had the other children to think about, too, especially

17-year-old Joe, who was to enter Howard as an undergraduate in the fall.

After discussing the situation with his family, Drew decided to delay his entrance into medical school for a few years. He would find full-time work in the interim and save his money. He therefore accepted a job as athletic director and instructor in biology and chemistry at Morgan College (now known as Morgan State University) in Baltimore, Maryland. He earned additional money by umpiring basketball and football games in the area. During the summer, when the college was closed, he managed the swimming pool at a junior high school.

By the summer of 1928, Drew had saved enough money to apply to Howard. His application was rejected, however, because his transcript showed only six hours of credits in English instead of the eight that the school required. A deeply dismayed Drew subsequently received an invitation from the Howard athletic department to become an assistant coach of the school's football team. But he was anxious to go to medical school and gave the offer little thought.

Instead, Drew applied to a number of other medical schools. A week later, he received a letter from Harvard University stating that his application had arrived too late for him to be admitted. If he reapplied the following year, the letter said, he would most likely be accepted.

But Drew was not eager to sit out another year. Fortunately, he did not have to wait very long for his wish to come true. He was at his job as pool manager when his brother, Joe, came running in with the news that Drew had been accepted to medical school by McGill University in Montreal, Canada.

Drew headed for McGill in the fall of 1928, abetted by several Amherst classmates who lent him money (at Tuss McLaughry's behest). He needed the extra funds because he was no longer living at home.

"Here I am: a stranger amongst strangers in a strange land, broke, busted, almost disgusted, doing my family no good, myself little that is now demonstrable," he wrote while in a low mood the following year. "Yet I know I must go on somehow—I must finish what I have started." To help cover his expenses, he worked part-time as a waiter.

In spite of his busy schedule, Drew still managed to join the university's track team. (Unlike graduate students in the United States, those in Canada are allowed to take part in intercollegiate athletics.) He competed in four events—the broad jump, the high jump, and the low and high hurdles—and was instrumental in helping McGill win several national championships. One of the top hurdlers in Canada, he became the country's all-time leading scorer in intercollegiate track competition. Moreover, when he was named captain of McGill's track team in 1931,

Drew (front row, center) at the age of 26, when he was named captain of the McGill track team. He went on to become Canada's all-time leading scorer in track on the collegiate level.

he became the first black American athlete ever to captain varsity teams at two major colleges.

Yet Drew's stay at McGill was not quite the same as his tenure at Amherst, where his emphasis had been on sports. At McGill, he proved to be an outstanding student. Early on, he was elected to Alpha Omega Alpha, the medical students' honorary scholastic fraternity. He won a $1,000 academic scholarship from the Julius Rosenwald Fund in his third year, and 2 years later he garnered the Williams Prize, given to the student with the highest score in an examination taken by the top 5 members of the graduating class.

Among Drew's favorite classes was An Introduction to Bacteriology, which was taught by John Beat-

Drew attended the medical school at McGill University in Montreal, Canada, from 1928 to 1933 and graduated at the top of his class.

tie, a visiting professor from England. One day, Drew was invited by Beattie to the pathology laboratory at Montreal General Hospital, where the associate professor of anatomy performed research on blood as part of his study of the essential nature of diseases. As Drew walked through the hospital's waiting room, he saw a group of worried-looking people sitting quietly in their seats. Doctors and nurses hurried back and forth through the wards. Drew found Beattie wedged into the corner of a room, busily conducting blood tests.

It was an unusually hectic day at the hospital, Beattie told Drew. Among the people in the waiting room was the family of an elderly man whose leg needed to be amputated. Beattie was testing blood samples from the man's relatives to determine their blood type. (There are four main blood groups: A, B, AB, and O. A person may give blood to and receive blood from anyone who belongs to the same group. Moreover, a person with type-O blood may give blood to someone whose blood belongs to any group, and a person with type-AB blood may receive blood from a donor in any group.) As soon as the professor found someone whose blood group matched the sick man's blood type, that person would be asked to donate blood for the operation.

Blood transfusion is said to have originated with the Incas in the 15th century, about 200 years before the technique was first employed in Europe. The first documented case of blood transfusion took place in 1667 and was performed by French physician Jean-Baptiste Denis, who used the blood of a lamb. In this case, as in most of those that followed over the next 200 years, complications developed and the recipient died.

Indeed, when incompatible blood types are transfused, the result can be quite dangerous. Because the donor's blood type does not have the same chemical makeup as the recipient's blood type, the latter may experience a high-grade fever, blinding headaches, and back pain. Sometimes, the blood plasma of one blood group clumps together and destroys the red blood cells of an incompatible group—an occurrence that can prove fatal.

Blood types were first discovered in 1901 by Karl Landsteiner, a Viennese-born pathologist who later became an American citizen and received a Nobel Prize for his scientific investigations. He managed to classify types of blood by noting the presence or absence of certain protein molecules on the surface of red blood cells. His findings not only ended the transfusion of incompatible blood types but made it pos-

sible for a recipient's blood to be categorized before a transfusion ever took place.

But Landsteiner's work did not ease the problem of acquiring compatible blood for a recipient. Doctors such as Beattie still had to test blood samples to find a suitable donor because there was no well-established method for storing blood. In 1835, T. L. Bischoff became the first person to perform a transfusion with stored blood. Similar procedures were performed periodically throughout the rest of the century.

The pathologist Karl Landsteiner, one of the most important pioneers in the field of blood chemistry, determined in the early 1900s that there are four major blood types. His discovery was instrumental in advancing the practice of blood transfusion.

Drew (back row, right of center) with the graduating medical class at McGill University in 1933. He elected to remain in Canada for the next two years and completed both his internship and residency there.

But blood banking failed to become a widespread process for several reasons. There was no known way to keep the stored blood from clotting. Neither was there a sterile method of storage. Nor was the means available to keep the blood adequately refrigerated.

A breakthrough in blood banking did not occur until 1914, when A. Hustin discovered that sodium citrate kept stored blood from coagulating. The following year, R. Weil pronounced that blood to which sodium citrate had been added could be stored safely for several days. But by the early 1930s, blood banking was still uncommon. To perform a transfusion, a doctor still had to locate a suitable donor. It was a time-consuming process.

Standing alongside Beattie, Drew watched the professor test blood sample after blood sample. Then a nurse came into the room and said that the sister of the man whose leg was to be amputated had arrived. It was hoped that she would have the same blood type as her brother.

Beattie asked Drew to draw a blood sample from the woman. When the professor tested the blood, the results were unpromising. Her blood type was incompatible with her brother's group.

Drew proceeded to withdraw some of his own blood. He gave the sample to Beattie, who found that it matched the blood type of the patient. A short time later, the operation was performed.

All told, Drew's experience at the hospital left him with a disturbing and important realization: Someone must discover a way to store blood over a long period of time. Precious moments were often lost as patients lay on operating tables waiting for donors to be found. Accordingly, Drew began to study the subject of blood preservation. ❦

4

CAREER OPPORTUNITIES

Drew GRADUATED FROM McGill University in 1933 and was awarded the degree of Doctor of Medicine and Master of Surgery. He subsequently served as an intern for a year at Royal Victoria Hospital and Montreal General Hospital. Then, in 1934, he became a resident in medicine at Montreal General Hospital, where he researched blood chemistry with his former professor John Beattie.

Drew's research was spurred by the work of several Russian doctors. He read an article about V. N. Shamov, who had postulated in 1927 that blood taken from a cadaver and mixed with a small amount of sodium citrate could be transfused with positive results. Drew also learned that three years later a physician named S. S. Yudin had proved Shamov's theory to be correct by successfully transfusing a cadaver's blood to a patient.

Drew began to wonder whether sodium citrate altered the blood's chemistry in another way. Did it affect the blood platelets—the saucer-shaped blood cells that are integral to the clotting process? Did the

In 1933, Drew (second from left) served as an intern at both Royal Victoria Hospital and Montreal General Hospital—a necessary step in his attempt to become a surgeon.

49

Drew (back row, center) at Montreal General Hospital, where he fulfilled his residency requirement, improved his surgical skills, and began extensive research on blood chemistry.

addition of sodium citrate to blood change the makeup of the erythrocytes—red blood cells containing hemoglobin, which transports oxygen from the lungs to the body's tissues? And did it affect either the protein in the blood that helps destroy bacteria or the opsonin—an antibody of blood serum that makes bacteria more susceptible to the action of phagocytes, a type of white blood cell that devours germs? Drew and Beattie used each other as sounding boards to consider these and other questions regarding the use of sodium citrate to prolong the shelf life of blood.

Their discussions did not last for long, however, because Beattie returned to London to continue his research on blood storage. Drew, for his part, attempted to gather all the information he could find on citrated blood. It seemed that most of the people who were researching blood storage were acting independently. Drew decided to sort out exactly how much was known about the subject by sifting through all the available information. He consequently spent a great deal of his spare time in McGill's medical library.

During his residency at Montreal General Hospital, Drew began to hone his surgical skills, and in time he became known as an excellent surgeon. In 1935, Canada's National Board of Examiners certified him as a surgical specialist. He was just 30 years old.

In the midst of Drew's accomplishment came the sad and unexpected news of his father's death, which was attributed to pneumonia. Drew returned immediately to Arlington, Virginia, to be with his family. His sister Nora and his brother, Joe, had become schoolteachers; Eva, soon to be 14 years old, was still in school. Their father's funeral was held at the Nineteenth Street Baptist Church, where he had sung in the choir every Sunday.

After the services ended and his family returned home, Drew announced to his mother, brother, and sisters that he had decided to leave Montreal and return to Washington, D.C. He wanted to be near his family, and he intended to accomplish that by becoming an instructor at Freedmen's Hospital, the teaching and clinical facility of Howard Medical College. After all, his excellent medical training would enable him to serve the school well.

The administrators at Howard University recognized Drew's value and hired him as an instructor in pathology for $150 a month, a relatively modest salary. The school, a private institution funded in part by the federal government, was anything but rich. Founded in 1867, it was named after General Oliver Otis Howard, who served as commissioner of the Freedmen's Bureau, an agency established by the U.S. Congress for the purpose of providing medical, educational, and financial assistance for impoverished southern blacks.

Freedmen's Hospital was founded in 1862—five years earlier than Howard University—to help treat the growing number of blacks who settled in the nation's capital during the Civil War. In 1869, the hospital moved to the Howard University campus and became the school's teaching facility. Freedmen's has remained associated with Howard University ever

An office of the Freedmen's Bureau, a federally funded welfare agency founded in 1865 to aid former slaves who lacked the bare necessities of life.

Daniel Hale Williams (shown here) was the first black to found a hospital in the United States. Shortly after he established Chicago's Provident Hospital in 1891, he was appointed chief surgeon at Freedmen's by U.S. president Grover Cleveland.

since. Today, it is one of the four busiest hospitals in Washington, D.C., and the third oldest. Moreover, the largest segment of black American healthcare practitioners in the United States are Freedmen's Hospital graduates.

The success of the hospital has been due largely to such people as Robert Reyburn, its chief surgeon until 1875, and Daniel Hale Williams, a black physician who performed the first successful heart operation. In the 1890s, Williams was summoned to

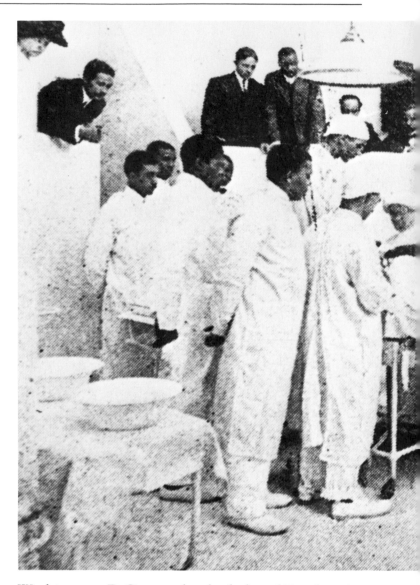

Washington, D.C., to take the helm of Freedmen's. He reorganized the hospital, recruited a staff of specialists, and started the nursing school. William A. Warfield, Sr., headed the hospital for the next 35 years—a tenure that came to an end just as Drew arrived. Numa P. G. Adams was the dean of the medical school when Drew joined the Howard faculty.

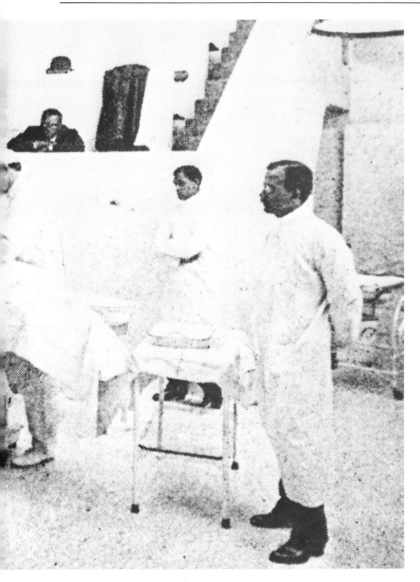

Freedmen's Hospital in Washington, D.C., where Drew became an instructor in 1935, was originally established as part of the Freedmen's Bureau.

Drew was well aware that black medical school students in the United States often encountered racial discrimination upon their graduation. As the *Saturday Evening Post* reported more than a decade later, "The openings available to the Negro student for his essential year of hospital training are in one or another of the country's 14 Negro hospitals approved for internships. . . . But if the young physician

Members of the nursing staff at Freedmen's Hospital (right and opposite), the teaching and clinical facility associated with Howard Medical College. Drew eventually became chief surgeon at Freedmen's.

wishes later to specialize, he will discover that hospital residencies—the chief avenue to specialization—are incomparably more difficult to obtain. If he practices in the South, he will find that he cannot treat his patients in the 'white' hospitals, even in the segregated wards."

Nevertheless, Drew made sure that his students worked hard and aimed high. "It is my belief," he said, "that surgeons can be trained at Howard to be as good as anywhere else." Accordingly, he adopted a paternal attitude toward his students. One of them,

Jack White, recalled that Drew's "main concern was our self-fulfillment. The last thing he said before I left for my residency was that, apart from my ability, he felt I had developed a very positive self-image which would stand me well in my relations with other people."

Drew was kept busy at Freedmen's. A free public hospital, it was obliged to accept patients from outside the city who were not permitted entry into the city's "white" hospitals. Thus, Freedmen's took in patients from Maryland, Virginia, and the Carolinas. Many

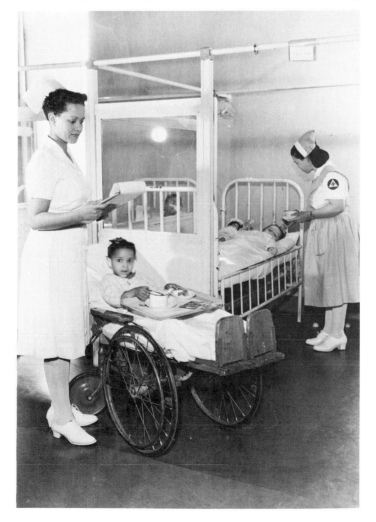

of them made it a special point to come to Freedmen's because of the hospital's excellent reputation.

In addition to teaching at Freedmen's, Drew continued his research on blood storage. He discovered that although sodium citrate has a tendency to destroy blood platelets, which are integral to blood clotting, the clotting process in patients occurred normally after citrated blood was infused. It was an odd finding—one that Drew continued to investigate.

In 1936, Drew was named an assistant in surgery at Howard Medical College and a resident in surgery at Freedmen's Hospital. The following year he became an instructor in surgery and an assistant surgeon. Then, in the midst of his teaching and research, a new opportunity came his way.

Drew offers instruction to the medical corps of the Office of Civilian Defense in the treatment of a patient (below and opposite).

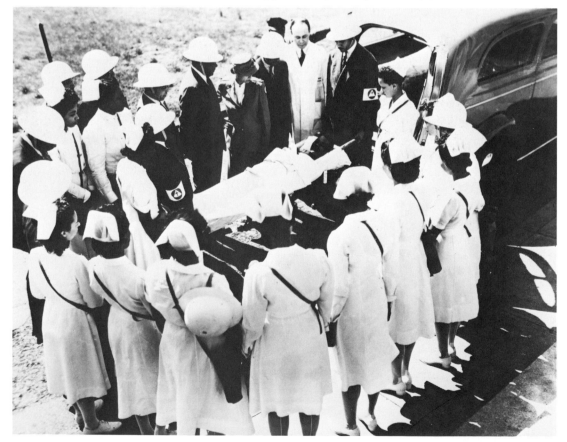

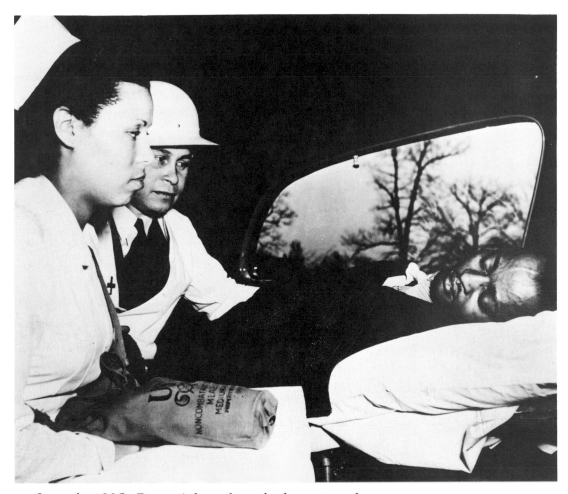

In early 1935, Dean Adams launched a series of discussions with the Rockefeller General Education Board, a philanthropic body, to establish a two-year fellowship for training outstanding physicians to head Howard's medicine and surgery departments. The funding eventually came through, and in 1938 Drew was offered a fellowship for advanced training in surgery at Columbia University Medical School and its affiliated hospital, Columbia Presbyterian, in New York City. He jumped at the chance.

5

SPECIAL ENGAGEMENTS

DREW ARRIVED AT Columbia University Medical School in 1938 and promptly became the first black in America to work toward the advanced degree of Doctor of Science in Medicine. Allen Whipple, the school's head of the Department of Surgery, assigned him to study under John Scudder, an assistant professor of clinical surgery who had been teaching at the school since the previous year. Scudder was in the process of researching blood chemistry, blood transfusion, and fluid balance—topics that matched Drew's interests—and the two surgeons immediately began to work closely together. In time, Scudder would call Drew "my most brilliant student" as well as "one of the greatest clinical scientists of the first half of the 20th century."

Drew's days at Columbia were busy ones. In the morning, he performed surgery; in the afternoon and evening, he carried out the research for his dissertation, "Banked Blood: A Study in Blood Preserva-

"Dr. Drew was naturally great—a keen intellect coupled with a retentive memory in a disciplined body, governed by a biological clock of untold energy," said John Scudder, one of Drew's professors at Columbia University Medical School. "A personality altogether charming, flavored with mirth and wit, stamped him as my most brilliant pupil. He had a flair for organization and attention to detail; he was a physician who insisted upon adequate control in his experiments."

tion," in a large, well-equipped laboratory at the medical center. As part of his research, he took blood from donors and siphoned it into a flask containing a solution of sodium citrate and saline. The mixture was then put into a container designed by Drew and refrigerated at a temperature of four degrees centigrade, which was supposed to keep the blood suitable for transfusions for up to two weeks. To warm the refrigerated blood when it was transfused, part of the intravenous tube through which the blood flowed was immersed in hot water.

Drew's research on citrated blood confirmed his suspicion that sodium citrate affected the blood's chemistry. He noticed that jaundice—a disease caused by an excessive breakdown of red blood cells, leaving a person's skin, tissues, and body fluids with a yellowish pigmentation—occurred in two patients who had been given blood that was more than nine days old. Consequently, he and Scudder decided to eliminate the use of sodium citrate in cases where a recipient was fighting an infection and a change in blood chemistry might prove troublesome. Scudder suggested that they give such recipients whole blood that included a chemical substance called heparin, which prolongs the blood's clotting time.

The next step in Drew's work was to help set up a blood bank at Columbia Presbyterian Hospital. In 1939, two years after the first blood-storage facility in the United States was established at Cook County Hospital in Chicago, Drew appeared before the Blood Transfusion Betterment Association, a medical organization that was interested in funding a blood-banking program at Columbia Presbyterian. He acknowledged to the association members that red blood cells began to break down after one week of storage and that banked citrated blood was not the same as fresh blood. Nevertheless, the positive aspects of stored blood far outweighed the negatives,

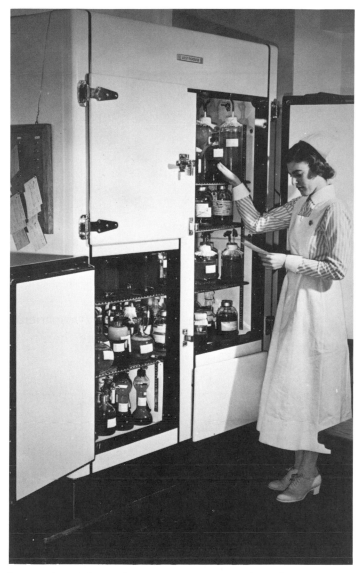

A refrigeration vault used for preserving whole blood. Donated blood can be kept for several weeks in such units if it is stored at a temperature between one and six degrees centigrade.

he said, adding that it was essential to have blood on hand for emergencies.

In August 1939, Columbia Presbyterian finally opened a blood bank. When it did so, the facility was under Drew's stewardship. He was named medical director of the program.

The establishing of the blood bank coincided with another special engagement in Drew's life. Several

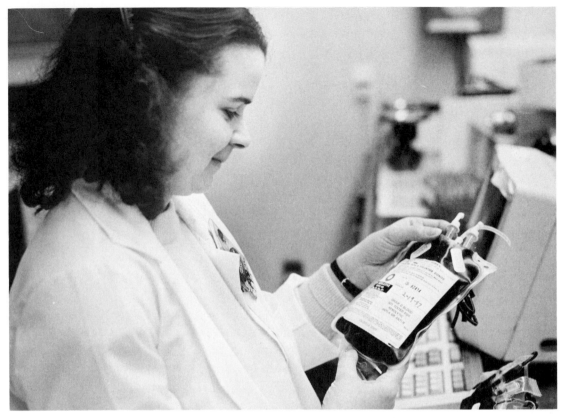

A unit of whole blood. Plasma, which contains nutrients, proteins, antibodies, and hormones, makes up about 55 percent of whole blood.

months earlier, in March, he had received an invitation from Numa Adams, dean of the medical school at Howard University, to attend an annual clinic at the John A. Andrew Memorial Hospital in Tuskegee, Alabama, later that spring. Blacks from all over the South were making their way to the clinic to receive free diagnosis and treatment.

In addition to examining the patients, physicians at the clinic also gave lectures. Adams asked Drew if he would speak at the clinic on blood transfusion, and the 34-year-old physician agreed. The trip would be a welcome break from his duties in New York and would give him the opportunity to see some old friends.

On his way south, Drew stopped at Arlington to visit his family. Then he and three colleagues from

Howard University drove to Tuskegee by way of Atlanta, where they stayed overnight. Drew decided to call on Mercer Cook, a fellow classmate at Amherst who was teaching at Atlanta University. Cook promptly invited Drew and his colleagues to dinner at his house. Among the guests was Minnie Lenore Robbins, a 28-year-old Philadelphia native who was a home economics teacher at Spelman College, the first school for black women in the United States.

Cook ushered Robbins over to Drew for an introduction. The young physician was immediately captivated by Robbins, and she was equally enchanted. She later said, "The moment I met Charlie I knew he was a man to be reckoned with—and the man for me."

Three days after he met Robbins, Drew left the clinic in Tuskegee and went back to Atlanta. His first stop was Cook's house to find out where Robbins lived. He was told that she resided at Bessie Strong, a dormitory for Spelman College's female staff.

Drew made his way to the Spelman campus well past midnight. Although the gate at the entrance to the school and all the dormitories were locked for the night, he was not deterred. He rang the night bell to Robbins's dorm and was met by a woman who refused to wake Lenore. But when Drew threatened to run inside the building and find her, the matron agreed to summon her.

Robbins was obviously surprised to see Drew. She was even more surprised when they sat on the porch and he asked her to marry him. Robbins protested that they had just met. But Drew persisted. He wanted an answer to his proposal that night, he told Lenore.

Robbins was not dressed for a long talk in the cold night air, Drew realized. All she had on was a nightgown and bathrobe. So he grabbed her hand, pulled her down the dormitory steps, and led her to the warmth of Cook's house, where they continued their conversation. The night ended with Lenore saying that a marriage between them was a possibility, but she was not yet willing to accept his proposal.

Drew continued his campaign to win Robbins's hand almost as soon as they parted, writing letter after letter to her. "I have moved through the days as one in a dream, lost in revery, awed by the speed with which the moving finger of fate has pointed out the way I should go," he told her. He wanted to become not only "a good doctor, and able surgeon" but "in my wildest moments perhaps also playing some part in establishing a real school of thought among Negro physicians and guiding younger fellows to levels of accomplishments not yet attained by any of us."

The letters worked. On September 23, 1939— five months after Drew first met Robbins—they were married in her hometown of Philadelphia. After the ceremony, the newlyweds moved into an apartment on West 150th Street in New York City. For the time being, taking a honeymoon was out of the question for Drew. There was a lot of work to be done at Columbia Presbyterian Hospital, especially at its newly established blood bank.

Much of Drew's research involved testing various methods of slowing the breakdown of red blood cells. Of all the methods he tried, the addition of sodium citrate to the blood worked best. Accordingly, he decided to focus on the citrate method and to experiment with different amounts of the compound.

Meanwhile, the hospital's blood bank was proving to be a huge success. Drew determined that the longest amount of time that citrated blood should be stored was one week. After observing 100 transfusions, he saw adverse reactions only in patients who received blood that was more than a week old.

Drew wondered if there was a way of salvaging the blood that had been stored for one week. It was of no use to him or his patients. All he did with the blood was send it to Karl Landsteiner, who used it in the experiments that led to the discovery of the rhesus (Rh) factor, a protein in the blood that is capable of inducing allergic reactions.

Around this time, Lenore told her husband that she had become tired of being a housewife. He was always heading off to perform surgery, she said, or doing research in the laboratory, or working on his

Drew performing blood research at Columbia Presbyterian Hospital in New York City, where he was a surgical resident from 1938 to 1940.

Drew preparing to examine a slide containing a blood sample.

dissertation, or attending to the small medical practice he had just started, whereas she always seemed to be by herself. When she suggested that she go back to teaching, Drew told her that he needed someone to help with his record keeping. Lenore agreed to be his assistant.

It was while Drew was explaining the function of blood and its components to Lenore that a thought occurred to him: Slightly more than half of blood consists of plasma, a fluid that contains nutrients, proteins, antibodies, and hormones. Red blood cells are the only components of the blood that break down after a week of storage, and there are no red blood cells in plasma. Moreover, plasma consists partly of fibrinogen, a protein that is essential in clotting, and the fluid does not have to be typed (because it does not contain any red blood cells). The more Drew thought about blood transfusion, the more he realized that plasma might make a viable substitute for whole blood. ❧

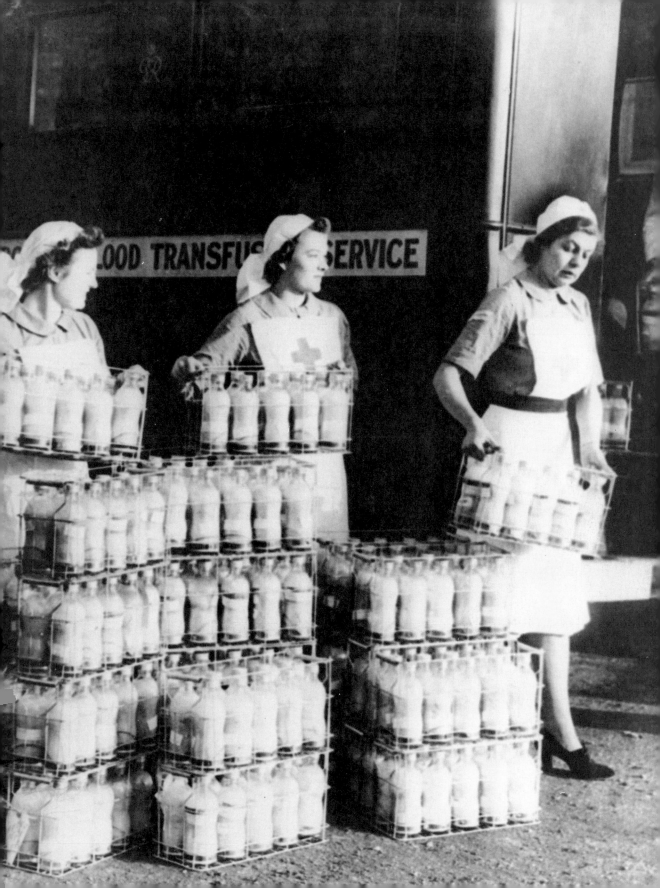

6

FINISHING
TOUCHES

❦

BY 1940, DREW and John Scudder were investigating the possibility of using blood plasma as a substitute for whole blood. In late April, they were asked to attend an emergency meeting called by the Blood Transfusion Betterment Association. Other experts in the field of blood preservation—including Karl Landsteiner and Max Strumia, the inventor of a machine that dried blood plasma—were there as well. Alexis Carrel, a Nobel Prize–winning surgeon and biologist from France, addressed the assembly. His countrymen, locked in a desperate fight against Nazi Germany, wanted the United States to set up a blood-banking program to aid the wounded French soldiers, even though America had taken a neutral stance on the war.

The committee members acknowledged that they were willing to help France. They pointed out, however, that the preserved blood would have to be used immediately because it had a storage life of about one week. There was also another large obstacle to hurdle. Blood types would have to be matched—a difficult and hazardous thing to accomplish on the battlefield.

Drew's work as director of America's Blood for Britain program gave rise to many scenes like this one, in which dried blood plasma, slated for use in blood transfusions, is loaded onto a truck in England.

Alexis Carrel received the Nobel Prize in 1912 for developing a technique that made it possible to sew the ends of blood vessels together. He was also part of a committee that launched a blood-banking program for France in 1940.

Someone suggested that medical teams be sent overseas to collect blood. France was organizing its own medical teams, Carrel acknowledged. But such a program was not enough. The need for blood was much greater than a collection program in France could address.

The problem seemed to defy a solution until Scudder was asked about the status of blood plasma research. He promptly turned the question over to Drew, who told the committee that his research on blood plasma had not yet led him to any definite conclusions. Nevertheless, the urgency of the situation seemed to dictate that plasma should be used.

Drew explained the properties of blood plasma to the committee and said that it was especially useful in cases of shock induced by burns or by a significant blood loss—the types of trauma that often arose on a battlefield. Unlike whole blood, plasma could be kept for as long as a month without being refrigerated. In fact, the plasma could be dried and transported from the United States to France and then reconstituted with sterile distilled water. The only drawback was that the procedure for drying plasma was as expensive as it was complex.

Drew added that he was investigating the possibility of freezing blood plasma. It appeared that frozen plasma would keep indefinitely. When needed for use, it could be quickly melted.

The committee members debated the advantages of using blood plasma rather than whole blood. Some pointed out that using whole blood was impractical, whereas others maintained that they should use a substance that they knew was safe. The overriding point, though, was that the situation had to be addressed quickly, and liquid plasma, which did not have to be refrigerated, was the easiest substance to use. Eventually, it was agreed that the United States would begin shipping plasma to France.

Drew and Scudder were named to a committee that was formed to oversee the operation. The first batch of blood plasma was scheduled to be shipped in late spring. But before the program could get started, France fell to Nazi Germany, and the project was scrapped.

Drew still had plenty of work to do. He was busy putting the finishing touches on his dissertation, "Banked Blood," which had taken longer to complete than he had anticipated. At one point, his manuscript contained as many pages as the New York City telephone directory. Allen Whipple, who headed Columbia University's Department of Surgery, told

Drew to cut its length in half. The dissertation wound up being 245 pages long and was termed a masterpiece by Scudder.

By the spring of 1940, Drew was also preparing for the oral examination for his doctorate. "His investigative work with Dr. John Scudder in fluid and salt balance studies, and subsequently in organizing the blood bank at the hospital, has been so outstandingly good that I feel he is entirely qualified to be examined for the degree," Whipple said.

Drew passed the examination with flying colors. "My work here is finished," he acknowledged to a friend after becoming a Doctor of Science in Medicine in June 1940. "I've gone as far as I can go in formal medicine, so I guess I'll have to go to work now."

Instead of enlarging his private practice, Drew promptly returned to Washington, D.C., where he received a dual promotion: He became a surgeon at Freedmen's Hospital and an assistant professor of surgery at Howard University. "No able surgeon has ever been trained there," he said of Howard, adding that "in American surgery, there are no Negro representatives; in so far as the men who count know, all Negro doctors are just country practitioners, capable of sitting with the poor and the sick of their race but not given to too much intellectual activity and not particularly interested in advancing medicine. This attitude I should like to change."

But by the fall of 1940—a month after the birth of his first child, "Bebe" Roberta (her nickname being the initials for *blood bank*)—Drew was back in New York, directing America's Blood for Britain program. His effort to set up a blood-banking program to aid wounded French soldiers had paved the way for his appointment to the post of supervisor. And he quickly showed himself to be a topflight organizer.

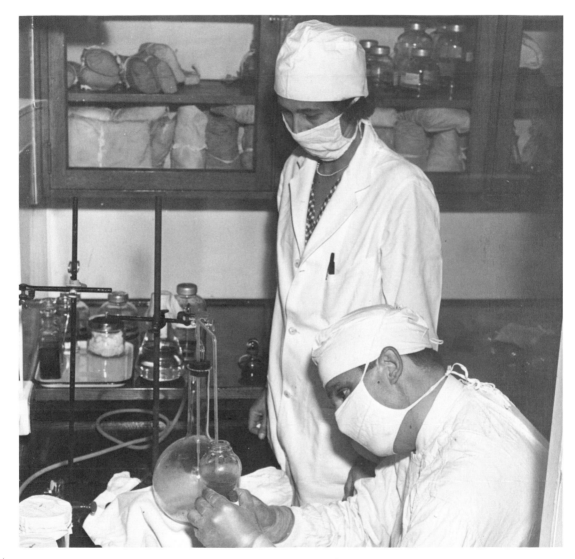

Drew assessed the problems with the Blood for Britain program and decided that to speed up the blood collection process the project needed a central location. After determining which hospitals were un-crowded, this main office would send donors to the appropriate blood collection facilities. He also di-rected that all blood plasma be tested at Columbia Presbyterian Hospital's bacteriological laboratory be-

In early 1940, Drew worked with John Scudder (foreground) in or-ganizing a blood-banking program to aid the French war effort. Scudder is shown here siphoning blood plasma into a bottle.

Members of the Red Cross, an international organization established in the 1860s to provide relief services for war victims, carry out their duties in London during the Blitz.

fore it was shipped out. To avoid the possibility of contaminating the plasma, only skilled personnel would be allowed to process it.

The Blood for Britain program ran successfully for five months. "Since Drew, who is a recognized authority on the subject of blood preservation and blood substitutes, and, at the same time, an excellent organizer, has been in charge, our major troubles have vanished," the Blood Transfusion Betterment Association officially stated. To top off matters, Drew wrote a final report on the project that summed up all the problems he had faced. The report later served as the guideline for similar programs established by America and its allies.

As soon as the Blood for Britain program ended, Drew joined the National Research Council and the American Red Cross in February 1941 in coordinating a blood-banking program for the United States. He insisted that collection centers throughout the nation set and maintain strict standards for keeping the blood plasma sterile. His goal was to have 1 million pints of plasma ready for immediate shipment, for it was becoming increasingly evident that the United States would be drawn into World War II. When that day arrived, America's blood banks would be well plenished.

While directing the national blood collection program, Drew attempted to perfect the use of human plasma. To separate blood plasma from red corpuscles, he employed a process called centrifugation. Whole blood was placed in a machine that impelled the plasma outward from a center of rotation and apart from the red corpuscles. Once this was done, he continued his research on manufacturing dried plasma. He worked on the problem over the next two months but was unable to figure out a way to mass-produce it.

By then, Drew was wrestling with another problem. In 1941, the U.S. War Department (later renamed the Defense Department) issued the following directive: "For reasons not biologically convincing but which are commonly recognized psychologically important in America, it is not deemed advisable to collect and mix caucasian and negro blood indiscriminately for later administration to members of the military forces." Shortly thereafter, Drew learned that

a number of southern blacks who were attempting to donate blood had been turned away from blood banks. Apparently, the armed forces wanted more than the segregation of "black" and "white" blood. They did not want "black" blood to be collected at all.

The rejection of blacks as blood donors reflected what was occurring throughout the military. Blacks in the army were being kept in segregated units, with

Drew with members of the American Red Cross. He worked closely with the organization in the field of blood banking.

little chance of being promoted to officers. In most cases, black soldiers were assigned to manual labor units after the completion of their training. Blacks in the navy did not have it any better. They were used as cooks and stewards. As a final affront, the air force and the marines did not accept blacks at all.

Drew denounced the blood segregation practice as insulting and unscientific. He was quoted as saying that in New York, at least, blood donations were accepted from people of all races. American Red Cross officials, acknowledging that the blood segregation policy being carried out was an attempt to appease the white American majority, quickly added that there was no scientific basis whatsoever for the practice of blood segregation.

Drew said as much at a press conference on the matter. "I feel that the recent ruling of the United States Army and Navy regarding the refusal of colored blood donors is an indefensible one from any point of view," he said. "As you know, there is no scientific basis for the separation of the bloods of different races except on the basis of the individual blood types or groups."

Drew (far left) in September 1940 with fellow members of Columbia Presbyterian Hospital's mobile blood unit—the first vehicle ever used to collect human plasma.

Human plasma is obtained by placing whole blood in a centrifuge, which whirls the blood at 2,500 revolutions per minute for 1 hour. This action causes the fluid part of the blood to separate from the corpuscles.

Amid this outcry, Henry Stimson, the secretary of the War Department, stated that the armed forces would remain segregated. Black combat troop units would continue to be commanded by white officers, and blacks would not be promoted to higher positions. "Leadership is not imbedded in the Negro race yet," Stimson argued.

Drew left the national blood program in April 1941, shortly after the U.S. War Department called for the segregation of "white" and "black" blood. He declared the announcement "indefensible" and stated that "there is no scientific basis for the separation of the bloods of different races."

In early April 1941, Drew resigned from his post as assistant director of the national blood program. Some people whispered that he had resigned because of his disgust with the practice of blood segregation. But as his wife, Lenore, later pointed out, "I'd never known Charlie to run from a fight."

Other rumors stated that Drew had decided to leave the national blood program for a more personal reason. Even though he had organized the mammoth operation, he would never be named program director because he was not white. Burke Syphax, a colleague of Drew's at Freedmen's Hospital, recalled, "Charlie was disturbed about the rumors, of course. But his returning to Howard was another thing entirely. There had always been sort of an unspoken agreement that he'd someday return as chief of surgery. It's a rule, so to speak, that we have around the school: the most promising of our surgeons is eventually offered the directorship. He always planned on coming back home." ❧

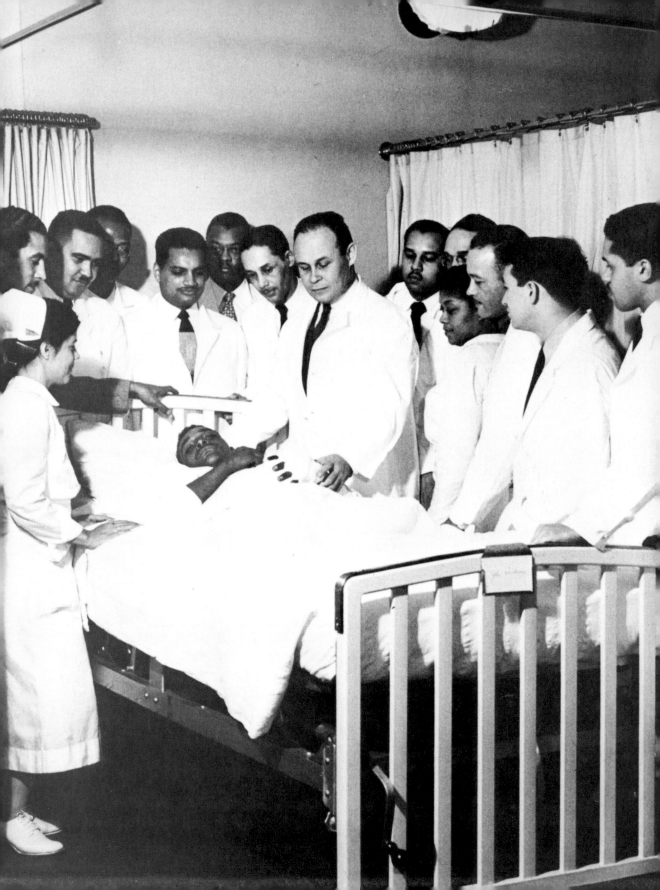

7

"THE REST IS YET TO COME"

SHORTLY AFTER LEAVING New York City in April 1941, Drew traveled to Johns Hopkins University in Baltimore, Maryland, to be examined by the American Board of Surgery for certification as a surgeon. During the examination, he was asked to discuss fluid balance in the human body, a topic he had been studying for years. His examiners were so impressed by his answers that at one point they called in other questioners to listen to his address. Drew not only was certified by the board but also was made an examiner later in the year.

In many ways, 1941 was a banner year for Drew. Upon returning to Howard University and Freedmen's Hospital that April, he was named professor of surgery at Howard and was appointed Freedmen's chief surgeon. His second child, Charlene, was also born that year. The Drews had two more children within the next five years: Rhea and Charles, Jr.

All told, the 1940s proved to be a decade of major accomplishments for Drew. While attending the John A. Andrew annual clinic in Tuskegee in 1942, he was awarded the E. S. Jones Award for Research in

Drew (center) with interns at Howard Medical College. "It is my belief that surgeons can be trained at Howard to be as good as anyone else," he maintained.

Medical Science. The following year, he was invited to join the American-Soviet Committee on Science. Freedmen's Hospital made him its chief of staff in 1944, the same year that he garnered the prestigious Spingarn Medal, awarded annually by the National Association for the Advancement of Colored People (NAACP) for the "highest or noblest achievement by an American Negro." Drew was the first physician and only the third man of science to receive the award. In 1915, the zoologist Ernest Everett Just became the medal's first recipient, and the agriculturalist George Washington Carver was similarly honored in 1923.

Despite these many achievements, Drew told a friend in 1944, "I feel that my life story as a physician has just had its preface completed and the rest is yet to come." Accordingly, he immersed himself in his work at Freedman's Hospital and at Howard, whose residency program was rapidly expanding. He was intent on improving the school's ability to train surgeons, and he used his contacts to get more funding and equipment for the university. Merle Hereford, who was a resident at Freedmen's Hospital under Drew, later said, "When Dr. Drew got with people, he made them believe things could be done that they just didn't believe otherwise."

Drew certainly thought highly of his students' abilities. In 1947, he wrote to Charles Cole, the president of Amherst College, "Since being here at Howard University most of our attention has been devoted to organizing the training system at first for surgeons, and later for all branches of medicine. At present, as Professor and Head of the Department of Surgery at Howard University, and as Chief Surgeon and Medical Director of Freedmen's Hospital, there is very little time for research, but the boys whom we are now helping to train, I believe, in time will constitute my greatest contribution to medicine."

The initial step in proving Drew's claim took place in 1948, when the first of his residents went to Johns Hopkins to take their examinations for certification by the American Board of Surgery. There was a lot riding on each of their performances. A failure to be certified would mean a huge setback for the black cause. If his students did not pass the examination, Drew knew it would be difficult to convince the heads of most hospitals that black surgeons

Drew and his wife, Lenore, attending a McGill University football game in 1944. "Sometimes I think I have lived down my career as an athlete," he said. "Now I have another problem. After all of my years of preparation for a practice in surgery I have become 'Mr. Blood Bank.'"

The scientist Ernest Everett Just was the first recipient of the Spingarn Medal, a symbol of black achievement bestowed annually by the National Association for the Advancement of Colored People (NAACP). Drew received the award in 1944.

were as capable as white ones. To add even more pressure to the situation, the performances of his residents would be measured against the test results of students from the nation's top medical schools.

Drew anxiously awaited word of the outcome. When the results were added up, two of his students scored higher than all of the others who took the examination. The occurrence marked the beginning of a startling string of successes for Drew. During the years that he remained at Howard, more than half of the nation's black surgeons who were certified by the American Board of Surgery were his students.

In fostering the first generation of black surgeons, Drew was clearly a demanding teacher. He maintained that when "one breaks out of this rather high-walled prison of the 'Negro problem' by virtue of some worthwhile contribution, not only is he himself allowed more freedom, but part of the wall crumbles. And so it should be the aim of every student in science to knock down at least one or two bricks of that wall by virtue of his own accomplishment."

But try as he might, Drew was not able to win all his battles. His biggest fight was when he took to task the American Medical Association (AMA), the nation's most influential medical organization, which was founded in Philadelphia in 1847 to provide continuing education for its members, represent them to the public, and act as a lobbying group before legislative bodies. He charged the AMA with setting up regulations that effectively barred blacks from joining the association.

Black physicians were not barred from the national organization. They were simply not allowed to join the ranks of many of the AMA's local chapters, and a physician had to belong to a local AMA chapter before he could become a member of the national organization. When a resolution was proposed in 1939, asking that "membership in the American Medical Association be not denied solely on the basis of race, color or creed," it was soundly defeated because local medical societies felt that such a resolution would interfere with "the right of selection of [their] own members, a fundamental principle in [their] organization." Washington, D.C., remained among the many cities whose local AMA chapter did not admit blacks.

Black physicians barred from local AMA chapters often lost patients to white doctors because they could not treat their patients in local hospitals. Moreover, many ill blacks elected to seek out white physicians rather than black doctors because of the hospital ban. Black physicians were outcasts in more ways than one.

In addition to its other activities, the AMA published a journal designed to keep its members informed of current developments in health care and research. Black physicians, including Drew, contributed to the *Journal of the American Medical Association* as well as other medical journals. According to W. Montague Cobb, who in the 1940s put together a bibliography of the contributions of black doctors to medical journals, blacks were permitted to publish in virtually every medical journal. His bibliography lists more than 2,200 titles by 650 doctors. Drew himself published 21 articles, mostly on blood preservation.

Yet, being published by an organization was not the same as being a member. Therefore, in January 1947, Drew sent a letter to Morris Fishbein, the physician who served as the editor of the *Journal of the American Medical Association.* Drew pointed out in his letter that the AMA had supported the District of Columbia medical society's action to bar black doctors from the local society 77 years earlier. This move automatically prevented them from ever joining the AMA.

"I shall not argue the question for admission as it stood in 1870, but I do feel that this age-long policy of discrimination under whatever guise or pretext is one of the dark pages in the history of an organization which otherwise has many bright ones," Drew wrote. His letter to Fishbein continued:

The men in Washington, the nation's capital, are still rejected although there can be no doubt of their qualifications by any standards, and so likewise are all the Negro physicians who happen to live in the South. . . .

At Howard University for many years no physician has been considered for a position of professorial or associate professor rank in the preclinical area who has not earned a Ph.D. in his special field. In Freedmen's Hospital, the teaching hospital for the clinical years, a man must have successfully passed his specialty board to be considered for the position of assistant professor. The chief of every department and subdivision in the department is a certified specialist in name and practice. Match these standards with those of the great hospitals of the land and they will be found good, but [the AMA] will not grant them the privilege of discussing common problems with fellow physicians in the learned councils of the American Medical Association now celebrating its one hundredth birthday. One hundred years of racial bigotry and fatuous pretense; one hundred years of gross disinterest in a large section of the American people whose medical voice it purports to be—as regards the problem of Negroes which it raised in 1870; one hundred years with no progress to report. A sorry record.

Drew went on to note that the American specialty boards accepted members on the basis of merit alone. The American College of Surgeons, he pointed out, had recently ridded itself of its policy of discrimination, measuring members solely by their ethical and surgical standards. Drew also pointed out that international colleges welcomed those of similar training and interests regardless of race or nationality. But not the AMA.

Drew chastised Fishbein: "If a small minority of county or state chapters persist in wagging the whole body, and the body as a whole makes no move to trust its own destiny, then it must be considered a body without true strength and purpose, or one which likes the way it is going. The American Medical

Editor of the Journal of the American Medical Association, *physician Morris Fishbein was a leading member of the powerful American Medical Association (AMA), a medical organization that effectively barred blacks from its ranks. In 1947, Drew launched an unsuccessful campaign to have blacks admitted into the association.*

Association should not start its second century with unfinished business of this kind, making mockery of its continuous protestations of leadership in medicine under the great and free American way of life."

The AMA's response to Drew was that "membership in the AMA is a matter determined by the local societies"—the old party line—so he wrote to the association yet again, telling them that their "by-laws can and, I think, should be changed." Despite his protestations, the rules did not change—not even in February 1948, when an interracial group of New York physicians started a movement for county medical societies in the South to accept black doctors. The group drafted a resolution to amend the charter of the AMA so that membership would not be affected by a person's race. The movement failed, however, and as a result Drew never became a member of the AMA.

In 1963, during the heat of the civil rights movement, a group called the Medical Committee for Human Rights (MCHR), which was set up to give medical assistance to civil rights activists working in the South, organized a large demonstration in New York. More than 200 physicians carried signs reading End Discrimination in Medicine Now along with Integrate All County and State Medical Societies as they marched outside the New York Coliseum, where the AMA was having its annual meeting. Despite this protest, the AMA failed to end racial discrimination by its local societies. The AMA would not put an end to the discrimination issue until June 1968—21 years after Drew's first letter to the organization. ✺

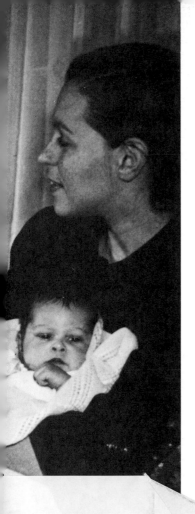

8

THE CONTINUING STORY

❧

I N 1949, DREW took, according to his wife, Lenore, "the first holiday he ever had." One of four physicians to be appointed as a consultant to the surgeon general of the U.S. Army, he embarked on a six-week tour of Europe, during which he investigated the medical standards at U.S. Army installations. The appointment marked the first time in American history that a black had received such a high-level, military-related assignment that did not have any direct relationship to black troops or personnel.

Drew made the trip a holiday of sorts by reserving hours for himself during which he pursued his of photography. When he returned to the he brought with him hundreds of slides. He ly invited friends to view them in the base-f his home at 328 College Street, on the How-iversity campus, and to hear his lecture on an architecture.

reshed by his trip, the 45-year-old Drew re-his many duties at Howard University and en's Hospital. But his schedule soon became

l his wife, Lenore, at home with their children (from left Rhea, Charlene, "Bebe" Roberta, and Charles, Jr.

extremely full. He served on the board of directors of the local branch of the American Cancer Society and on the board of trustees of both the National Polio Foundation and the National Society for Crippled Children. He chaired the surgical section of the National Medical Association and also did work for the Young Men's Christian Association. His wide-ranging efforts helped put to rest negative thoughts in the white medical community about the abilities of black Americans.

At home, Drew received phone calls at all hours of the day from his patients. He always made sure to give them as much attention as they needed. "He was driven by his dream," Lenore said. "It seemed that all alone he had taken on the incredible task of changing the world."

On most evenings, Drew would come home after working all day in the hospital and collapse into a chair. On one occasion, his daughter Bebe came to him in tears, holding a rag doll whose head had come off. Drew directed her to fetch his doctor's bag. The "patient" required "surgery," he told his daughter.

Drew took out a curved needle and some sutures and proceeded to reattach the doll's head to its neck. When he finished with his sewing, he pulled on the sutures and expertly tightened the stitches. "He had all the instincts of a good parent," Lenore maintained. "He didn't have much time, but he gave [the children] his fullest."

Freedmen's Hospital took up the bulk of Drew's time. In its survey of hospitals and health conditions in Washington, D.C., the Washington Metropolitan Health Council reported that the medical care at Freedmen's was "of a high professional grade and the administrator is far-sighted and well informed. . . . The institution is impressive in spirit, its volume of work and its many evidences of progressive, forward-looking policies." In fact, another

Washington Metropolitan Health Council report found that the infant mortality rate at Freedmen's was half that of nearby Gallinger Hospital, a whites-only facility.

As Freedmen's chief surgeon, Drew also represented the hospital at a number of medical conferences, including the annual free clinic at the John A. Andrew Memorial Hospital in Tuskegee, Alabama, which he had been attending since 1939. Shortly before the 1950 Tuskegee clinic took place, Drew decided to drive to Alabama rather than fly so

"If we take care of education," Drew said, *"race will take care of itself."* He is shown here at a Howard University speaking engagement in late March 1950, two days before his fatal accident.

This portrait of Drew, presented in 1959 to the American Red Cross, is still on display at the organization's national headquarters in Washington, D.C. At the dedication ceremonies were (from left to right) Drew's brother, Joseph; his sister Nora; his mother; his daughter "Bebe" Roberta; his sister Eva; and American Red Cross president Alfred Gruenther.

he could travel with three other physicians—Samuel Bullock, John Ford, and Walter Johnson—and save some money.

The four men agreed to take turns driving Bullock's black Buick Roadmaster. They left Washington, D.C., on April Fools' Day—a Saturday—shortly after 2:00 A.M. Bullock was the first driver. Drew, who had spent most of the previous day and night in the operating room at Freedmen's and attending a Howard University student council meeting, volunteered for the second shift. He settled into the back seat and slept until it was time for him to drive.

Drew took his turn behind the wheel in the early morning hours, shortly after they reached Richmond, Virginia. He made a rest stop near the Virginia–North Carolina state line, then resumed his place in the driver's seat, with Bullock seated next to him. Drew was still piloting the Roadmaster along North Carolina State Route 49 when, at close to 8:00 a.m., a few miles north of Haw River, the car began to veer off the road. "All I remember is suddenly coming awake and noticing that the sky wasn't exactly where it ought to be," Bullock recalled.

Drew had momentarily fallen asleep at the wheel. Bullock yelled out, "Hey, Charlie!" waking Drew, who immediately tried to straighten out the car. But it went off the road instead and continued on to a field, where it turned over three times before landing right side up.

When the car came to a stop, Johnson got out of the back seat and helped free Bullock, who was wedged against the dashboard. Like Johnson, he seemed to be all right. The only injury he had sustained was a cut hand. Ford had been thrown from the car, but he appeared to be in relatively good shape, too, suffering only a broken left arm.

Drew, however, had caught his right foot under the brake pedal, so instead of being thrown completely from the car, he had been trapped in such a way that the vehicle had rolled over him. When the others reached him, he was just barely alive. His left leg was nearly severed, and his body was in shock.

An ambulance arrived. The attendants put Drew inside and took him to the Alamance General Hospital, an old facility in the nearby town of Burlington. Three doctors attempted to revive the noted physician. Their efforts included giving him a blood transfusion, but nothing they could do was of much help. Two of his veins that return blood to the right atrium of the heart had been badly damaged in the accident, causing him to hemorrhage internally.

About an hour and a half after he first received medical attention, Charles Drew died. He was 45 years old.

A wake was promptly held for Drew in a chapel at Howard University. Funeral services were observed on April 5 at the Nineteenth Street Baptist Church. The mourners included Allen Whipple, John Scudder, and many of Drew's patients. Mordecai Johnson, the president of Howard University, said in his eulogy of Drew, "Here we have what rarely happens in history . . . a life which crowds into a handful of years significance so great men will never be able to forget it."

On the same day as Drew's funeral, about 20 of his friends instituted the Charles R. Drew Memorial Fund. Part of the money collected for the fund helped provide for his widow and four children. The balance was used to continue the research projects initiated by Drew and to establish scholarships and lectures in his name.

Indeed, Drew's legacy has grown over the years. Not only has the quality of human plasma used in transfusions been improved, but, thanks in part to his research, certain proteins that are found in plasma have been employed in new ways. Albumin, the most plentiful protein in plasma, has an ability to attract water, and it is now used to reduce excessive swelling that occurs in tissues outside the blood vessels. Gamma globulin taken from a donor immune to certain diseases (such as measles) can transfer temporary immunity to those diseases to the recipient. Fibrinogen, a protein that is instrumental in blood clotting, helps stop bleeding during long surgical procedures.

Drew's pioneering work in blood plasma helped these discoveries come about, and his efforts have been duly acknowledged. Schools and hospitals have been named after him. His portrait hangs in the American Red Cross's national headquarters in Washington, D.C. Another portrait of Drew can be seen in the National Portrait Gallery and yet another in the Clinical Center of the National Institutes of Health in Bethesda, Maryland. Unveiled in 1976, it marked the first time that a portrait of a black American was included in the institute's gallery of distinguished scientists.

That same year, the Charles R. Drew Commemorative Medal was established to honor exceptional achievements in the advancement of the medical education of black Americans and other minorities. The first medal was struck two years later and was given to Drew's widow. Inscribed on the back of the medal were the words:

> Dr. Charles Richard Drew devoted his life to mankind both as a scientist and teacher to many aspiring black doctors. His pioneering crusades in blood research led to the use of plasma during World War II and also to the establishment of the first Blood Bank in the United States. His dedication and enthusiasm to the field of medicine shall be remembered by all.

Another tribute came in 1981, when the U.S. Postal Service issued a commemorative stamp in honor of Drew's contributions to science.

Nevertheless, some of the lore surrounding Drew remains untrue. Shortly after his funeral, a rumor began to spread that a whites-only hospital had refused to admit him because he was black. According to this story, America's pioneer in blood preservation subsequently bled to death.

Bullock, Ford, and Johnson—the three black doctors who were at the hospital with Drew—all stepped forward to dispute this statement. "A conscientious effort was made to revive Dr. Drew," Johnson and the others claimed. Nevertheless, the story of Drew bleeding to death was picked up by such

IN MEMORY OF
CHARLES RICHARD DREW
1904 — 1950

CHARLES RICHARD DREW
1904 - 1950

BLACK SCIENTIST AND SURGEON

PIONEER IN THE PRESERVATION OF BLOOD PLASMA

MEDICAL DIRECTOR OF THE BLOOD-FOR-BRITAIN PROJECT, 1940

DIRECTOR OF THE FIRST AMERICAN RED CROSS BLOOD BANK, 1941

TEACHER TO A GENERATION OF AMERICAN DOCTORS,
FREEDMEN'S HOSPITAL, HOWARD UNIVERSITY, WASHINGTON, D.C.

OUTSTANDING ATHLETE, AMHERST COLLEGE AND McGILL UNIVERSITY

MEMBER OF OMEGA PSI PHI FRATERNITY

STEADFAST FOE OF RACIAL INJUSTICE

DIED IN ALAMANCE GENERAL HOSPITAL, 1 APRIL, 1950,
AFTER AN AUTOMOBILE ACCIDENT AT THIS SITE

A marker erected at the site of Drew's fatal accident in North Carolina features a bronze plaque that lists his many accomplishments. At the unveiling of this marker in 1986 were (from left to right) his brother, Joseph; his daughter Charlene, and his wife, Lenore.

periodicals as *Time* magazine and the *New York Times*, which was still reporting more than 30 years after the auto accident that "the segregated hospital to which he was taken had no blood plasma that might have saved his life."

It is not known exactly when or where the myth surrounding the circumstances of Drew's death began. In any event, the story of an unjustly treated Drew helped him emerge as a symbol to all black Americans whose civil rights have been restricted because of their skin color. Even today, the myth still adds fuel to the burning issue of equal opportunity.

Yet Drew's actual contributions do not need any embellishment. Not only did he leave behind a legacy of pioneering work that made possible the preservation of blood plasma and the establishment of blood banks, but he also helped prepare a new generation of physicians who carried on his research. "There must always be the continuing struggle," he said, "to make the increasing knowledge of the world bear some fruit in increasing understanding and in the production of human happiness." Drew himself attempted to do just that. Indeed, few men of science have served the public as conscientiously or as nobly as did the physician, educator, and research pioneer Charles Drew. ❧

CHRONOLOGY

1904   Born Charles Richard Drew on June 3 in Washington, D.C.

1922   Graduates from Dunbar High School

1926   Graduates from Amherst College; becomes athletic director and instructor in biology and chemistry at Morgan College

1931   Named captain of the McGill University track team; joins the Alpha Omega Alpha Honorary Medical Society; awarded a grant from the Julius Rosenwald Fund

1933   Awarded Doctor of Medicine and Master of Surgery degree from McGill University

1934   Becomes resident in medicine at Montreal General Hospital

1935   Certified as a surgical specialist by Canada's National Board of Examiners; becomes an instructor in pathology at Howard Medical College

1936   Named assistant in surgery at Howard and resident in surgery at Freedmen's Hospital

1937   Becomes an instructor in surgery at Howard and an assistant surgeon at Freedmen's

1938   Awarded a fellowship for advanced training in surgery at Columbia University Medical School

1939   Named medical director of the blood bank at Columbia Presbyterian Hospital; marries Lenore Robbins

1940   Awarded Doctor of Science in Medicine degree by Columbia University; becomes an assistant professor of surgery at Howard and a surgeon at Freedmen's; directs Blood for Britain program

1941   Helps the National Research Council and the American Red Cross coordinate a blood-banking program; certified as surgeon by the American Board of Surgery; named professor of surgery at Howard and chief surgeon at Freedmen's

1942   Awarded E. S. Jones Award for Research in Medical Science

1943   Joins the American-Soviet Committee on Science

1944   Made chief of staff at Freedmen's; awarded Spingarn Medal by the NAACP; named chairman of the Surgical Section of the National Medical Society

1946   Becomes a fellow of the International College of Surgeons

1949   Tours Europe as surgical consultant to the surgeon general of the United States Army

1950   Dies in car accident near Haw River, North Carolina, on April 1

FURTHER READING

Bims, Hamilton. "Charles Drew's 'Other' Medical Revolution." *Ebony*, February 1974.

Bittker, Anne S. "Charles Richard Drew, M.D." *Negro History Bulletin* 36 (June 1950): 144–50.

Cobb, W. Montague. "Charles Richard Drew, M.D., 1904–1950." *Negro History Bulletin* 42 (July 1950): 238–46.

Drew, Charles. "The Role of Soviet Investigators in the Development of the Blood Bank." *American Review of Soviet Medicine* 1 (April 1944): 360–69.

Drew, Charles, D. Stetten, C. P. Rhoads, and J. Scudder. *Report Concerning the Project for Supplying Blood to England.* New York: Blood Transfusion Improvement Association, 1941.

Drew, Lenore Robbins. "Unforgettable Charlie Drew." *Reader's Digest*, March 1978.

Hardwick, Richard. *Charles Richard Drew: Pioneer in Blood Research.* New York: Scribners, 1967.

Hepburn, David. "The Life of Dr. Charles R. Drew." *Our World*, July 1950.

Lichello, Robert. *Pioneer in Blood Plasma: Dr. Charles Richard Drew.* New York: Simon & Schuster, 1968.

Parks, D. "Charles Richard Drew, M.D., 1904–1950." *Journal of the National Medical Association* 71 (1979).

Pringle, Henry, and Katherine Pringle. "The Color Line in Medicine." *Saturday Evening Post*, January 24, 1948.

Scott, C. W. "Biography of a Surgeon." *Crisis*, October 1951.

Wynes, Charles E. *Charles Richard Drew: The Man and the Myth.* Urbana: University of Illinois Press, 1988.

INDEX

PICTURE CREDITS

ROBYN MAHONE-LONESOME teaches at a public elementary school in the Bronx, New York. She received a B.A. in English from Spelman College in Atlanta, Georgia, and earned an M.A. in Afro-American studies and an M.S. in journalism from Boston University. Her articles on medicine and education have appeared in the *New York Times*, and she has also written for the *Boston Bay State Banner* and the Brooklyn *City Sun*.

NATHAN IRVIN HUGGINS is W.E.B. Du Bois Professor of History and Director of the W.E.B. Du Bois Institute for Afro-American Research at Harvard University. He previously taught at Columbia University. Professor Huggins is the author of numerous books, including *Black Odyssey: The Afro-American Ordeal in Slavery, The Harlem Renaissance,* and *Slave and Citizen: The Life of Frederick Douglass.*